Paul Savoie

Crac

Translated by Donald Winkler

BookLand press

Published by BookLand Press
15 Allstate Parkway, Suite 600, Markham, Ontario L3R 5B4
www.booklandpress.com

Printed in Canada

Library and Archives Canada Cataloguing in Publication

Savoie, Paul, 1946-
[Crac. English]
Crac / Paul Savoie; translated by Donald Winkler.

Translation of: Crac.
Poems.
Issued in print and electronic formats.
ISBN 978-1-77231-023-8 (paperback).--ISBN 978-1-77231-024-5 (epub).--ISBN 978-1-77231-025-2 (pdf)

I. Winkler, Donald, translator II. Title. Title: Crac. English

PS8587.A389C7313 2016 C841'.54 C2016-900013-3
C2016-900014-1

Canada Council for the Arts Conseil des arts du Canada

ONTARIO ARTS COUNCIL
CONSEIL DES ARTS DE L'ONTARIO
an Ontario government agency
un organisme du gouvernement de l'Ontario

We acknowledge the financial support of the Government of Canada through the National Translation Program for Book Publishing, an initiative of the *Roadmap for Canada's Official Languages 2013-2018: Education, Immigration, Communities*, for our translation activities. We acknowledge the support of the Canada Council for the Arts, which last year invested $153 million to bring the arts to Canadians throughout the country. We acknowledge the support of the Ontario Arts Council (OAC), an agency of the Government of Ontario.

To Claire

table of contents

lower depths 7

screen 39

crac 89

lower depths

it hits you full in the face

a door opened
backwards
shutters the livid wind
lashes with the purest rage
of a whip-wielding wind
bestriding its four chariots
in a furious race
from its epicentres out

or would it be the tsunami
that teases the ankles first
then with its voracious tentacles
tugs towards the open sea
thrusts into its black hole
into its gaping inhaling maw
with the teeth that chew shine chew
and the ravenous devouring mouth
all within reach
it can find

and works the flesh
as one rips to shreds
a recalcitrant hunk of meat
then swallows
making sweet spirals
in the Adam's apple

coiled serpent
spin-drying the belly
and the ventriloquists taking shelter there

a mighty machine to contort
whatever worms its way
by hook or crook
into its ken
mowing down
all in its line of fire

would it be a huge machine's
forked tongue
in the lower depths
that sucks
tugs
clutches at what passes near

like an overturned geyser
spilling its guts
into the bowels of an earth
on fire
with a core that writhes
seethes
heaves down from below

lava underfoot
leaving one to totter
hobbling along
over shifting surfaces

surfaces with distorting mirrors
turbid waters
crystalline pale
as if all could be reflected
while nothing casts back
the suppliant face
backed by the beautified bluish
sky
so truly returned
to its own beginnings

nothing harks back to anything

there are only numberless
surfaces
reduced to a single smooth
surface
unendingly polished
insolent
delinquent even
because it makes as if to humour you
glides you along

when your foundering's all it knows

the polished skis
on which to keep one's balance
and glide
and endlessly surf
on this surface without end

not to fall
nor to mar the surface
nor split the epidermis
as one would hack at an arm
a leg
a neck
with blows from a pocket knife newly honed

and if this body were left
on its well-tutored ski
now bereft of the undulatory art

to falter

trip up in the cylinder

leaving abrasions of blood
on its own numbed
shell

under the bloodied wave
the serpent becomes all the serpents
of all the lower depths
all that moves
beneath docile surfaces
lying in wait for what limps   reels
swoons

to then embark
on the beautiful zigzag dance
of all that stirs
and entwines

the low is one with the high
the foot with the arm
the head masquerades as coral
the lips open wide their cleft
to let the sea horse flee

then solitary
uncertain
the ride begins

fingers claw at the clotted scabs
mistake the fins' fury
for a maddened immersion

the only bulwark
this side of darkness
the heart of the drowning
hub of the whirlwind
the end of words
a stammering

the end of tears as such

the end of who might have crept
to the horizon
from the opposing side
of what's just at that instant
disclosed
too weak to reach out

powerless to fold in
to hold tight

what no longer sees more
than the underside of things

the plausible locus of a convulsion
if not a barrier
to push back all
the opposite way

and if the door stopped banging
so angrily
in what's left of a beating heart

if the shutters
whipped by an inscrutable wind
and that go crac crac crac
if they were to pound less hard

yet batter away still
with what's blowing in
like something unhinged
come from who knows where
but near impossible to hear
so much does the speed of sound
garble doubly triply all

so much do all noises
merge into one

to take in every tangled surface

as if all could
come together
produce the same effect
upon a house that barely stands
so much does the door slam closed
ferocious
so much do the hinges fold in on themselves

so much does everything bang away
relentless

these noises
in the end
strike full in the face

the rustling
even the cries
the groans
have been wrung dry

still there remains
the whirlwind

all that's left
is this hyphen

which has you thinking of silence

and its twin inclination
to intrude itself
and become a simple parenthesis

lying in wait for what's in the wind
or perhaps playing it up

with the same promise of force
yet resigned to whiling away time

wedged in between what's no longer done
and what one dares no longer do

happy no more
with what came before

we await the worst
each one assailed
by fresh anguish

that is to say an infernal noise
barely resembling a noise
but that still torments

assaults what's left of your throat
your gut
your breath

the hoarse cry persists
makes you wish
despite the missing body
muscles
nerves
to cry out louder than those numberless
murmurings
that take themselves for dying falls
while knowing only now how to deafen

beneath this surface
where nothing resembles anything
and nothing conjugates to the end of time

the silence into which the seahorse would intrude itself
with its androgynous dreams
creature of the lower depths
barely able to afford itself an algae
a lichen

with hardly enough strength
to process the wave
and its infinitude

what the beast's tail
leaves in its wake

a tiny current at the end
of a long dwindling line

a sheaf-shaped
stream

an ear

played out like a week beam
deep in a cavernous night

what's afoot in the air
alights on the hand
perhaps even a finger's tip

just painful enough
for this stirring
to be felt through what's left
of the body

just stubborn enough
to coax one more spasm
from the murky surround
to disrupt what up to then
beneath the hurting surface
dared no more to flaunt
the diminutive dance

what in the lower depths
would dare the vital entwinement
would curl up tight
to the serpent's coil
with barely the strength to bind
the wish to devour

having no more strength
to grapple
with the void

anchored in you
in the doleful sea

weary

so profoundly weary
smitten with its own torpor

there where you lie
dead drunk
the living dead

seeking the nerve
to risk again
to take on
the shadow's deceit
the ineluctable force
of the seed-bearing ear

to flee
before the doleful outpouring
over the expanse
thus fractured
by this sad
and implacable
rush of water
upon what's left
of the shore

to redeem the village
the people who vanished
beneath the wave's
unflagging force

and of whom we find
no trace

beyond the echoing
of a sea
that now draws back
before what it has just devoured

water that strikes
the reef
again and again
to the end of time

screen

the blue dictates all
you just must refrain from desire
from thought

let the blue
cover you over with deep lines

folds of furrows

where is nested all you will become
all you dare not to be
outside yourself
beyond this fragile shell

that you confer on the place
on the field of play
like blood
decanted from needle to needle in a vacuum
to pour out your heartbeat
on what is done
what makes of you
something other

something bloodless
dwells in you
decanted
a daguerreotype
of what each one lets drop
to add to what fails to be

advance

retreat

there

right in the middle
of a sphere
that doesn't even claim
to be a circle

but a concentric action
a circle's simulacrum

a pebble that could make for a widening
of what the first annular impulse
imparts to the surface

a surface that's calm
crystalline
that the palm leaf encloses
in a move
to stave off dilation

to scatter wide
what the crystal
gathers in
from the turbid deeps

the crystal entraps
contains
only contains

the surface frees itself
from every depth
yielding to the laws
of diminishment

the vanished shores
at the heart of all confinements

the sheet of slate
as first principle
issues from a stiff blow
razing to the ground
sweeping clean
where the tidal wave comes in

this within each concentric
movement
between what the pebble affords
to vastness
and holds back
pending an act to be performed

an act in the making
its spark
its manifold path
like a beast
lord at once
of a thousand lairs
forcing its claws
deep down

the bite like an opened valve
a shutter dumbly offered to the wind
like a mouth that breathes in
the void

strip away the avid aperture's husk
ponder the sky
the ground
the root

suck on sap
blood that spurts from another
like an eruption

of what the earth
rebuffs
throws off

from deep in its entrails

volcano of doubtful eruptions
bedded in what in the end sets nothing free
just spews away
burns with a fire
the flame flees

here
everything's injected

you're the needle
the syringe
up against the tendered skin
you're what works its way in
punctures

collapses the conduit

skitters
every which way at once

reach out the arm
stretch taut the skin

towards what beating thing?

what organ
in thrall to breath?

you proclaim in a half-stilled voice
the edict of being

here

in a circle
that takes itself for nothing other
than a circle's absence

you make the first move
there

or there

it's of no importance

make a clean slate
or else you'll cave in
to the core of this curious world
down onto strange carpets
giving no hint
of footprints

the steps are taken elsewhere

far from the precise point
where you find yourself

never in exactly
the same place

your arm
starting from the wrist
traces an arc
to a thousandth of a thousandth of a centimetre
of the wished for curve

it takes flight
like one condemned to death
who one might think to have broken free
bound for the outer limits
of what confines it
forever

nothing eludes anything
only endless arcs exist
and the bisecting line

the rod that splits in two
multiplies   divides
superimposes

the rectangle inside the rectangle

hold the expanse's infinitude
within reach

bird-catcher
you snare the eagle
forever renewed
by your own flight

you break away

your body
your veins
cease to weigh on your brain

you map out your own territory
you clear a path

you shift course
or something of the sort

there

it's a wrap

you let yourself drop
roll
you roll over yourself

three times
three times three
again and again
it's done
Bob's your uncle

and you pop up somewhere
on a screen

the screen gathers you in
the blue wraps you round
you roll in it
like the fruit that splits
to enfold what's inside
a heart-shaped
pit

the organ beats

beats
far from your lips
which an ancient savour perturbs
a trace of old saliva

what you breathe

taste
what your lips
savour no more

no longer knowing
the shape the pit takes
when the juice veers
volcanic

and your tongue
for the body
lays down a limitless line
over the fleeting beauty
of desire

taste one last time
the mimesis
of a holy fire
in what might have been

flame that the tom-toms
no longer excite
surfaces
no drum can trouble

roll
let yourself roll

pivot

reform the arc
starting with the other still point

the one at the nth degree
of your contortion
your superb turning back on yourself
in the arc a thousand times learned
that the body executes
on a high wire

balance the body
over the extinguished
falls

the curbed furrows
of Niagaras
at the tips
of unlaced feet

there is nowhere
to plunge
no net with outstretched arms
to break the fall

fall anyway

it's the only way to be

a fall
that has nothing to do
with your toppling body

with what the margin marks out
as a beginning

what the imagined line limns
as an end

in the midst of many surrounds

you don't even feel the breaking
of your bones
the ruckus is somewhere else

you have only to let the screen be

fall
as if it had nothing to do with you

fall
as if remote from the act of self-torment
of hurting
of feeling bad

for the next scene
when you pierce your heart
with a sharp blow come from away

your face is blank

you wear the mask
of what every damaged visage
knows of pain

imprint
catchment for a tear
an abrasion
what grasps cuts
slashes

the crease in the making
the clouding of brows
the wide-eyed stare
the fawning
the fear

all that

and nothing of that

above all don't move

don't raise
your brows

your face is a dash
the eye but a hyphen
the forehead
a space
between two phonemes

search no more for words
words exist no more

there's nothing to say

nothing is said

silence is all

the sentence is spoken elsewhere
differently

just listen to your lips
your row of teeth
the palate
the tongue

the vowel's shape
a sequence of syllables

what's being hatched
what's in the works

a sentence
or what brings it to mind

no need to recreate
the mouth's precise shape
your mouth in particular
dictates all
while imparting nothing

you've nothing to add
nothing to subtract

all is absorbed
into what's not said
what is said no more

does there exist a game of love?
an abstract for acts of love?

you are embraced
you embrace

what arms enlace you?
what makes you tremble so?

all may be consumed
is consumed
you bequeath to the still point
your act of enfoldment

you enfold the void
as a spellbound child
reclaims the air-strewn
bubbles

or snares with a net
dragonflies suddenly there
over a vast field

that exists

or is on the verge
of existing

the field invents itself
as it goes

the net removes itself from the scene
you reclaim it
it's restored to you a hundred times
a thousand
right on the spot
then slips away again
from your very hand
its tensed grip

you end up undoing yourself

your body
the particular shape of your body

so it would seem

here
now you remember
there are only arcs

what comes just before
what follows

and the blue
so much blue

goblet blue
cistern blue
blue that nibbles
blue that gobbles

blue into which you insert yourself
as in a jar
that eeks its way in

commit yourself to blue
its rules
its edict

become the blue
its bones
its blueprint without end

descend into it

only the surface counts
the pebble
with its concentric movement
in zones of unending blue

blue to on high
blue to below

shutter against the wind

crystalline blue
that attracts
captivates
captures

run
until breathless

fleeing felon
fly to the open sea
far
from this crystalline blue

that snares you
even where flight
holds sway

turn in circles
your body's length
the length of your arc

of the reach
of this circle
that never becomes
a circle

never stops
not being

blue shutter
whose slats are flown

an old fashioned bird-catcher
that takes wing
lets itself soar away

an instance of what opens
and closes
at the same time
forever

crac

on my old wooden chair
blotched with blue and white stains
seated in front of my terminal

I plug into the planet's
wavelengths
messages rain in
like shoot-out
shells

who are they firing at, anyway?

they come in at an unthinkable speed
I have too few messages in me
to answer all that arrive
in a whirlwind
as they say

time bombs

because everything is said
but almost nothing gets through

it's a window on the world
I'm assured
meaning I'm in a house
or something like it
a shut-in place at least
one that contains me
enables the coming in and going out
of what issues from me
explains in a certain sense who I am
which I perhaps invent as I go along

because nothing
can wholly exist here
nothing with its own realness
one that's authentic

all is transformed
just as it's taking shape
as if a word
after leaving the mouth
says something different
when it grazes the mouth of another
who receives it and lobs it back to me
without my being able to recognize the source
the business perhaps starts with me
but returns to me like a wave
from the middle of a stream
that has somewhere lost its way

then when it reaches shore
you look far off
to see from where the movement comes
but you wonder towards what sheen of water
you've just veered

the reflection looks like something else
not at all what you supposed
not quite
what was there at first

not precisely
what was there
before

if I'm really and truly in a house
or a shelter
when the words pass through the window pane
they just skim the skin
give me a shiver
but if I look up
at the path they took
I see that rather than slipping in
they've punched all asunder

everywhere there are holes

beams pass through thicknesses
to target the skin
and no doubt flay it

I lift an arm to shield myself
but the shafts still find their way
through the carapace

what ought to serve as a wall
is riddled with holes
clefts
breaches that shed no light
send back no image
the opposite way
towards what now seems beyond bounds
virtually unreachable
so much does what permeates the inner zone
deeper still draw me down

I sink
but I don't feel
that it's into myself
but towards something else
I cannot name

towards what?
towards whom?

a loud noise
makes itself heard
a noise that goes crac
the sort of rumble
that augurs an earthquake
a fracture you feel approaching
from deep in the ocean
the earth's core
and that mounts mounts
spreads itself wide
in the wake of the great fault spinning out hither and yon
over all the planet
like a comely web
spun from the entrails of an abhorrent bug
from a god perhaps
with nothing better to do
than to blow up all that strays
into his field of fire
he takes a malicious pleasure
in exploding from within
or without
all that claims
to have justified its existence
but that can't now remember
why it took such pains
to raise up this stronghold
this rampart that now guards
against nothing
to dig this moat
become
like all trenches
one more trap

trenches that rather than laying on limits
rip them down
it's from there you take aim at the enemy's ground
its stockade
and you find yourself targeting
together
all enclaves
wanting to level
all fortresses
so much does the margin you've just put in place
move out
like so many arteries
over the earth's surface
while no longer freeing up anything at all

once the centre no longer holds
and the surge bears you away
there's nothing to be done
but to let yourself drop
beneath the tidal wave

the water that strikes
delivers one more crac
the only sound left
we don't quite know
if it's the last sound now
of the earth's pulse
that of a heart in its last gasp
left to grab on
to whatever's within its ken

the water strikes
that's all we can say
for sure
and hauls beneath its bulk
what dares to pit itself
against the roaring
immensity

there's one kind of imprint left

the only name one's able to give
to what
remains

a remnant perhaps

does it finally lend
to the cramped
confines
the strength for renewal
that of a wheel that turns
from its centre?
or is there no more left in its viscera
than the wrenching out
of the world's root?

the noise assails me
pummels me
drives me back
to what's left
of the wall

how to vanquish
what gnaws
from within
and pecks away
at every periphery?

what sort of cry can resist
the wailing
that subdues
and devours?

I'm up to here with waiting
bloated with ruins
ready to burst
with laughter broken out in bleached out sprouts
on my skin

I remain
famished
thinner than ever

inconsolable too
before the bruised fruit
served up
by so many unruly
hands

they open me up
to a world
that shuts down on me
stop opening me
onto what one barely remembers
having closed

this morning
a frigid morning
one of those winter mornings as frigid
as all those I've known
since I landed on earth
one beautiful frigid morning
not long after the War
the most frigid in this century
of grand fratricides

this morning I rage
I toss my good French out the window
and I say to all those sons of bitches
with their know-it-all ideas
only good
to make us crawl a bit more
to make us prance
dance to their tune
like marionettes

there's someone going to rage against me
maybe my father
the principal
the judge
the priest
the office de la langue française
all those who slam the door
when it suits their purpose
but I don't hear them any more
they've pissed me off enough
with their rules
as though life wasn't regimented enough already

it can't go on like this
there has to be a limit
to being taken for a sucker
being stepped on
even after all those hungry years
after we showed we weren't like before
we weren't just voyageurs
for a national holiday
lumberjacks
raftsmen
big boozers
guys only good for taking it easy
laughing too loud
smashing in faces after the midnight shift
at the tavern on Friday
cursing more richly than the night before
then coming to Sunday Mass all beat up
all contrite
because you hadn't been good
not a bit wise
almost not Catholic
to be bawled out again by the priest
who says you've got to do better
you shouldn't let yourself be had
by the bad guys across the river
the other side of the border
who'll take away
all our money
our past
our land
our women
our children
our grandchildren
and leave us nothing

nothing at all

mustn't let yourself be had
mustn't let yourself be duped
again
like all those times before
since when they sang to us
that we didn't win
that famous battle
on that bloody plain
that I'd like to bury ten thousand feet underground
so they couldn't still make us bleed from old sores
and I don't mean just those
who call themselves victors
so they never again make me get down on my hands and knees
to say thank you for their not having ravaged my guts
not having thrown me again against the wall
not shot off guns in my face
to make me stop bellowing
once and for all

seems to me
I've been sounding off for so long
that I don't know any more
what I'm bitching about
what I was insisting be done more
better
different
and to whom I was spouting so many idiocies

I let others speak for me
and they went off looking
for something that didn't change a thing

so I find myself
right in the same place
as if I were still starting out
and all kinds of things have been stripped away
with just about nothing
added on
and I still have to ask
why I'm here
and what you want from me

they tell me
that it's maybe my fault
I didn't send the children to a good school
I didn't punish them enough
harden them enough
defend our territory enough

I'm fed up
having to come out
of my own hole
the one that's mine
without being mine
it's because of me
even if I'm not guilty

so whose fault is it?

this time
I'm not going to be had
I'm going to say something
I'm going to break a chair
smash some glass
throw the furniture out the window
sometimes that does you good
to get rid of all you've got
make a clean sweep
empty out everything all around
it gives the impression
that you can
muster new blood
and begin again
right from zero

as long as that bloody zero
doesn't just stay put

and you can graft it
onto something
that makes some sense

well tonight
I need a good dose of zero
even if it's liable
not to heal my hurts
with a new beginning showering down
like on the seventh day
that's also the end of a really important deed
a vast project to put things in their place
the end included

but really
what came before?

it's not the real end
because everything that comes before
serves as a prelude
for everything that comes after
except you don't really know
what use it is
to have taken so much trouble
to have racked your brains so long
to end up there
and make a world
that always ends up being the beginning of a world
the beginning of a world
you never end up building
or never end up understanding
what it's all about
that construct in which you live
why you shaped it that way
it seems so stupid sometimes
so lacking
so appallingly incomplete
that it gives you goose bumps
so much you can't imagine
how you're going to live within it

and I say to myself since forever
that it's up to me
to see where I stand in all this tralala

it's not their fault
if I can't adapt

I'm an oaf
if I think the world around me
is going to make the least effort
to bend to my demands
to conform even a little
to my idea
of a place
of a spot
where I'd like to live

that's not the way
things go

it's never
like that

I want nothing to do
with a land that's not a land
I'm fed up with the winter
they want to stick me with
like a bloody obligation

my country's not winter
but a land
that asserts itself
despite winter

between a big snow drift
and a sky so blue
that from time to time
it just feels good
to lose track of the north

don't tell me to clear out

I'm not leaving this place

I'm planting my stake even deeper

don't ask me
to dress up in old costumes
to pass the pipe around
to beat a beat-up tom-tom
there's no more sacred dance
in this circle too often laid waste
there's no more echo
in this acoustic
too dense
with silence
and misunderstanding

I'll dance as best I can
I'll move about as best I can
in the constricted round
of my steps

on a path
not very well
cleared

they won't be able to say of me
"he doesn't know
what foot to dance on"
I dance on my two feet
in the eternal square dance
I've been taught so well

in the lovely jig
of ancient times
reimagined
a reel
more real
than the virtual images
on your screens

I dance the dance
of him who stands fast

I don't cave in
I don't walk out on you

don't tell me any more to go live with you
I'm staying home
this is where I live
I'm not one of yours
but rather one of mine
I feel good
on this land
as badly defined
as a gesture far off on the plain
a territory both open
and closed
which is mine

I am the plain
it is me

you don't rob a plain
of its dust
nor its wind

you don't conjure a land like that
with beings to people it
just to go and live elsewhere
later

not really

do I belong
to a people
have I a heritage?

what will I leave
to my children?
to my grandchildren?

there are only faint signs
I have no hieroglyphs
I have no caverns or castles
I have only small bungalows
with wooden siding
or stucco
most often worn down
or faded
poorly maintained
little streets that may twist and turn
but for the most part make perfect rectangles
and end up most often
at a riverbank
along a waterway that doesn't feed much any more
now so black or brown or filthy
that nothing would dare mirror itself there
or find its likeness within

I'm a guy of the plains
a nomad man

moving around doesn't spook me

itinerancy is my disguise
the better to live
in a fractured space
that mends itself in me

I will live there

you'll not be able
to do away with me
to wipe me off the map

even if I live woefully in my place
and if my place fits poorly
onto the map
even if the millenary human swarm
makes of my vital zone
an ill embraced space

I'm not going away
I won't disappear

I'm not an invisible man

I won't be wiped off the slate

I'm here

here I remain

about the translator

Donald Winkler was born in Winnipeg, graduated from the University of Manitoba, and did graduate study at the Yale School of Drama. From 1967 to 1995 he was a film director and writer at the National Film Board of Canada in Montreal, and since the 1980s, a translator of Quebec literature. In 1994, 2011, and 2013 he won the Governor General's Award for French to English translation, and has been a finalist for the prize on three other occasions. His translation of Samuel Archibald's short story collection, *Arvida,* was a finalist for the 2015 Giller Prize. He lives in Montreal, Quebec.